AT THE FOOT OF THE CROSS
REFLECTIONS FOR GOOD FRIDAY

KEVIN CAREY

STATIONS OF THE CROSS ILLUSTRATED BY KEVIN SHEEHAN

Sacristy Press
PO Box 612, Durham, DH1 9HT

www.sacristy.co.uk

First published in 2016 by Sacristy Press, Durham

Sacristy Limited, registered in England & Wales, number 7565667

British Library Cataloguing-in-Publication Data
A catalogue record for the book is available from the British Library

ISBN 978-1-910519-34-9

www.jesus4u.co.uk

CONTENTS

PREFACE

When I sat down to write a set of reflections on the Stations of The Cross specifically for Good Friday 2010 I found myself almost overwhelmed by the weight of my own Passiontide history, itself only a scruple compared with the weight of a tradition of piety in words, painting, sculpture and music almost entirely based on the Synoptic tradition and, necessarily, denying itself any hint of Easter; but I found myself deeply stirred by a growing consciousness of the Johannine tradition, reflected to a considerable extent in Luke, which speaks of how Jesus never lost control of his situation. I therefore resolved to write two reflections for each station, the first, more familiar, based on Mark and Matthew, the second Johannine and perhaps a little challenging, sometimes verging on the triumphalist. Some will find the two accounts uncomfortably dissonant but I hope that many will find them profoundly contrapuntal.

These reflections, with a period of silence after each, were written to occupy two hours. At their first delivery, each was followed by a half verse of the Stabat Mater (Attrib. Todi, Trans. Caswell; Tune Stabat Mater) and while the material of the reflections and hymn did not correspond, it was felt that the music broke up the continuous speech otherwise only interrupted by periods of silence. The insertion of the hymn necessarily shortened the periods of silence.

Ideally, the two "voices" should be taken by different readers, one gentle in tone for the Synoptic voice, the other more definite in tone for the Johannine.

These Reflections are dedicated to Michel and Val in whose house they were begun, and to Richard and Storm in whose house they were completed.

Kevin Carey, *Penhurst, Feast of St Martin of Tours 2009*

I. JESUS IS CONDEMNED TO DEATH

i.

Guilty!
Not a patrician vote from the Senate floor
but a dithering Governor,
damp-handed, petrified in the stony gaze
of frightened men, hardened and fore-shortened by the Law.
Guilty with all the countless victims
     pincered in the law's bent vice,
the desperate propitiation, calamity delayed
for another day with a pointless sacrifice.
Oscar Romero shot, peasants with no name,
scapegoats with momentary, violated fame.
Children forced to carry guns and children shot
for what they and their killers had forgot.
Boots on gravel, boots
kicking down the door;
I stand with them as the dark strikes four
and officials indifferently record,
and men wearing weapons as casually as eye
     glasses ceremonialise a judicial kill,
the public facelessness of the public will.
From the whispered threat to the whispered accusation,
I know the story, the chronic subterfuge and temporisation,
the callous calculation;
the man must die for the people,
the man must die for the law;
the over-turner of tables in the Temple
must learn what sacrifice is for.
And I stand with a sense
of only half wonder

that the street demonstration has dissolved,
that the rhetoric of the challenge is a victim of the challenge,
that the tactics of temporary withdrawal are innumerable.
for in spite of the bonhomie on the boats and
      the comradeship of the road
and the bright hope when a leper croaked with amazement,
I was always lonely;
not God-lonely but man-lonely, world-lonely,
always seeing past the talk and the spasm of bravado
into the gap I came to fill.
"My Father's will," I thought, and, then, less certainly,
"My Father's will."

ii.

Guilty!
At last, the necessary ordeal is radically foreshortened:
I was a judge in the hall of judgment,
mockery simply a parody turned back on the mockers;
in the garden I frightened the soldiers;
at the ill-assorted farrago of inquisitions
      I asserted his my kingship;
all they could do was demean themselves in charade,
that cloak and knee-bending burlesque;
and the mighty man of Rome asking "what is truth?"
When all he was called to act upon was proof.
Yes, I will be with them, the down-trodden and the persecuted,
I will be in the cattle trucks and the death camps,
clutching my gas mask in the trenches,
standing beside them in the firing squad,
but not only in the person of the human Jesus

but there to lift them to myself as God.
I watch the hurriedly disappearing figure of Nicodemus,
off on an errand of reconciliation;
I watch the Governor hurriedly wiping his
    hands on the inside of his cape;
I see Peter, ruddy and rudderless, reeling, making his escape;
and I see the temporary truce between
    the officials and the soldiers
dissipate, poisoned by its casual misuse;
and I see that when they have all gone back, down-hearted
into their accustomed occupations,
they will find me again. I am the one
they will all depend upon.

II. THE CROSS IS LAID UPON THE SHOULDERS OF JESUS

i.

Weighed down,
the wood of all the world
set on my slender shoulders.
Weighed down by a life of wear and care:
my mother and family, the disrupted, disoriented disciples
and the blight of the bloody shadow spreading
across the beloved, gentle sea of Galilee;
and the care of the countless sisters and brothers
who weighed down the boat
and sat on the mountain grass
for the word of life and the bread of life
and those who took a risk with the palms and the shouts of
Hosanna!
And the care of the countless I knew,
the faithful, sacrificing Jew
and the strangely prescient few in Decapolis.
Let it weigh me down,
let it weigh more than I can bear,
let it contain within its cast-off wood
all the earth's pain and care;
now is the time to carry and to share, to suffer and to bear.
There is no better place than here
for all the cowardice and fear,
for the deed half-wrong, for the word half-true,
for the friend half-gone and the self half-known,
for the place you stood, saying you could not follow.
If there was heroism it has gone now:
you have not followed,
I can scarcely lead;

but there is this sense in me of the dogged,
the supporter of Galilee United through
    much more thin than thick;
the fire of Isaiah in my bones
and the long, slow trajectory of Jeremiah.
Lay the burden, the out-cast wood
on the outcast Northerner;
for some of them will remember that I was out-cast
for doing good.

ii.

Weighed down
by this outcast wood,
I flinch, then flex, straighten my knees and stand,
to bring all earthly forces into my command;
they shall not mourn, they shall not speak
of loss as this last journey sings:
Lift high The Cross.
I bade you come to me,
all you that labour,
whose burden laid you low,
and I would lift the burden from your shoulders,
leaving a load which you could bear for me,
conferring, in God's grace, love's dignity.
Do you remember Lazarus?
Or has that fame been lost
in the mayhem of ritual and politics?
Has it become, in the propaganda of the establishment,
another of my inexplicable sacred tricks?
Or does it reach forward into this final, earthly dawn

when I shall complete the mission for which I was born?
Watch how the dawn breaks in this last day
when I shall walk the crooked, human way,
look at the dawn against whose roseate light
you see The Cross set high,
above humanity.
Look at its stark, black limbs
against the sky,
source of derision to all those who pass by,
but source of all hope for those who watch and pray,
for those who do not flinch, who do not turn away.
Prepare to follow where this wood must lead,
to death which overcomes all human need.

III. JESUS FALLS FOR THE FIRST TIME

i.

Limb-locked
I hit the stony ground, knees grazed,
hands numb as the cross piece staggers down
the crazed hill.
In the moment before organisation catches up with events,
I see snatches of a rush mat let down through the tiles;
and the sad man trapped at the pool-side who almost smiles;
and the woman bent double.
There was always so much unlocking to do,
of the physical and the mental,
of the self-inflicted and the moral:
unlock those doors, unlock the laws,
unlock the guilt, unlock the love.
So much to unlock which Cousin John called sin
but it was more often the case that people needed to be unlocked
from themselves so that they could let God in.
A priest passes, so close
that I admire the fringe of his robe.
How I made fun of them and look where it has led.
It does not do to unlock the law
or it pours out in untidy pieces
and spreads itself across the marble floor:
a piece for the accountant; a piece for the handmaid;
a piece for the goldsmith; a piece for the marriage broker;
yet pieced out, not amounting to much,
a mosaic puzzle with its own odd symmetry and coherence
but what has that to do with God?
I am not sorry that I unlocked the law;
and such a nice fringe.

With a stroke of startling, sadistic expertise
the soldier's knotted stick unlocks my limbs
in searing release
and I crawl to the halted cross piece.
Unlocked, the blood pains as it courses.
There is something about the indifference
        that sustains a kind of survival,
Unlocking can be painful.

ii.

Impassive,
I stand in the turmoil, my load laid down
to watch the best and worst of humankind
thronging the narrow street:
a disciple momentarily appears at an impossible angle;
traders stand full-shouldered against the
        human tide pushing up the hill;
a mother weeps her children away from the gruesome drama;
an old woman my hands unbent scuttles past
as if nothing is happening,
as she did at the time, as if her unbending was normal;
incongruously, a musician asks me for a donation;
a priest glides by, gorgeous and aloof
and I have to resist the temptation to bar his way
and ask him: "What is truth?"
He sees the stand-off between the Temple
        Police and Pilate's cohort
and wants none of it.
The crowd presses as if it is driven by an
        inner, collective compulsion,

not so much blood lust as a need to get this over with
in order to get on with the next thing.
Strange that my people who are longing for the Messiah
have no way of recognising the real thing.
At last the soldiers become restive
and one strikes me with his stick
and, so as not to seem docile,
I calculate the time between the blow and the time to go.
I say a prayer, remembering Zechariah
and lift The Cross a little higher.

IV. JESUS MEETS HIS BLESSED MOTHER

i.

Mother
of watchfulness, mother of woe, impassive, transfixed
in an upper window.
Ever resourceful, how did you get up there?
I watch my footing for a moment and, looking up,
there is nothing.
I watch my footing again and, looking up,
she stands before me,
crying, pleading for something,
torn from a tableau, turbulent in her own torment and time.
That it should come to this:
all the strange magic of the stable and the shepherds
and the kings and the elders in the Temple;
and the strange, miraculous happenings;
and the crowds finally bursting in
Hosanna!
And yet it has come to this;
that a mother should suffer the worst fate,
watching her own son into the grave
while she has to wait.
But she knew all the time - like
most of us, domesticating the warning -
of the old man saying - as she told it, reluctantly
when I was leaving home -
that she would suffer for me.
I say: "Mother" and she says: "Son";
and I say: "You know it was meant; the Prophets foretold".
"Yes, the death of holy heroes,
not of grieving mothers, growing old".

"I will be with you, mother."
"I know, sweet Jesus, on your golden throne;
but I will miss the muscle and the bone."
Then, seeing a blow descending,
she half turns with natural modesty
and, with a mother's face, losing all self-absorption
smiles that smile, she only kept for me.
Then she turns and weeps when she thinks I cannot see.

ii.

Mother
Queen of Heaven, blessed mother,
she looks upon my passion with a pain like ecstasy,
sings her soul a faultless threnody,
hymns the climax of my peerless agony.
She looks as if to speak,
then knows how this would break the sacred thread;
she looks as if to touch, to move a lock of hair
from my wounded head,
knowing that her touch will charge her dread.
The boundless comfort of mutual silence;
then she flinches as a fly settles on an open wound,
then re-composes herself;
she is the only one at present,
as I stand,
who sees past the scars and sordid treachery
to the glory wrought in me;
what sweet sadness, what necessary searing,
what serene agony,
what sublime endearing.

I turn my face to the madness of the crowd,
to the turbulence of the people:
to the hatred so hot that it is almost inarticulate;
to the suffering so deep that it falters into monotonous keening;
to the stolidly blank,
weighing out parched corn as if nothing were happening;
to the children chasing an orange down the slope,
getting entangled in my feet;
and to the soldiers pushing against them up the winding street.
I walk this way for something better for all of these;
and, as most of my beloved friends have fallen away,
only she knows now what they will know
when the Pentecostal wind begins to blow
and the Pentecostal flames begin to glow.
Hail! holy Queen of Heaven,
unlike any other born of woman,
blessed mother.

V. SIMON OF CYRENE IS FORCED TO CARRY THE CROSS OF JESUS

i.

Foreigner!
Lynch him!
Dog, you will find our sticks persuasive,
our swords flashingly eloquent.
See this other dog!
Bring him to his place of death.
Fierce and resentful, he turns where they cannot see
to the source of his humiliation;
then his face softens.
What does he see in me?
A torn traitor?
A lashed liar?
A scourged scoundrel?
He sharply calculates the aggression over his left shoulder.
"You are that sweet Jesus that rode on the ass,
that unlocked the law,
that gave hope to the poor.
I heard the story from Decapolis
of a woman who out-witted you on behalf of all of us.
We have eaten the crumbs from under your table
but now I am carrying it in a strange reversal of fortune.
If I bear this weight from this rubbish-choked brook
to that place up there where the poles rise stark,
then I, not the Jews, will have carried the wood of the Cross
and the table of your sacrifice."
I think I follow and smile encouragement.
"Come now, sweet Lord;
pretend to take the weight.
As a seller of spices I am not too strong:

one pace for the suffering;
one pace for the poor;
a third for the widows;
a fourth for the weak;
a fifth for the cowards;
a sixth for the meek;
a hill for the helpless;
a climb for the stricken;
a journey for the feckless;
a destination for the broken.
Come on, my sweet Jewish foreigner."

ii.

All the world
arrives to view my Passion,
no longer a Jewish internal affair
but an act of global, eternal destiny. They have seized a man,
they say of Cyrene,
black as Moses' Ethiopian wife
and, without knowing, they weave him into my life.
As I stand and wait for them to agree the new arrangements,
I think of Isaiah and how my story is like his story,
except that he could not have imagined a
        gentile carrying this cross;
we have reached, in words he would not have said,
a tumultuous watershed.
Simon carries the cross for world history
that will bring countless to love my Father,
brought through me.
I let him lift the dead wood in my stead,

just for a moment bearing all the weight,
to symbolise the world as it will be.
He sings a counting song,
leggier in metre than the curt-cropped Psalter,
richer than the clean-limbed counting
as the nets came in,
smoother than ever the wheel turned as the rope strained,
full of strange sadness,
long notes thrown upwards,
then slowly curving downwards to the earth.
He looks over his right shoulder,
then takes my hand:
"It's not what I would have chosen
but, pardon the imposition,
it is staking a kind of claim."
Feebly, I squeeze my affirmation.
As the pulse ebbs,
as the blood disarrays,
he is the whole world now, grown small,
to share my Passion plays.

VI. VERONICA WIPES THE FACE OF JESUS

i.

Broken
the face, the keen toned lines distorted,
the crown cut deep,
the bone's lament,
the blood dividing skin into a jagged maze;
the liveliness drained down to the death of movement.
The eyes still live,
limply, limpidly, in recess,
the only loving organs left to encourage and caress.
Again I miscalculate the height of a stepping stone
and lose momentum,
then blunder into an oasis,
a courtyard on the way to nowhere,
lost to the crowd, the barging and heckling,
feeling the last caress of the cool morning.
A woman dressed like a waitress, with a linen
        cloth over her extended arm,
counts the places at an empty table
and smiles with tavern charm;
and then, turning to pass back, she sways out of dead reckoning
and presses the unfurled cloth against my face,
cool as the spring.
Just for a moment, we see my face as if reflected in a pool.
Broken, broken,
it has come to this.
She hovers between my face and its image on the cloth,
then imprints my imprinted lips
with a parting kiss.

Sometimes in the evening, I thought, when the
        fire burned low and the men fell
into habitual solemnity,
they will forget the joy of the tavern,
the kissing and the drinking;
they will too easily think
that I came to love the serious and the dry,
forgetting
how they were when the boats came in,
before they thought I wanted them to be religious
and warriors against sin.
I wonder if they will ever regain the capacity for joy,
the pleasure in the dance, the solace of the bottle,
the birth of an unlooked-for boy.
So it is well that I receive my last act of kindness in a tavern yard
and leave my face on a wiping towel.
Time please, gentlemen,
time please,
no more now, save your breath.
Think of the joys of Bacchus
and the pain of death.

ii.

Look upon the wounds of glory
printed on a sacred shroud;
look upon the face of Jesus,
quiet before the roaring crowd;
look upon the scars of rapture,
look upon the wounds of power,
see the majesty of suffering,

pictured in its final hour.
Look upon the maiden gentle,
tending to that sacred face,
look upon that naive kindness
blind to horror and disgrace;
look upon her simple solace,
in a moment's graceful care;
see her looking at his image
like a lover, gone, but there.
See this face near death encaptured
like the sculpture and the coin;
but this is our king forever,
his the everlasting throne:
see the noble scars of triumph
borne victorious to forgive;
see the glory in the pathos,
life in death that we might live.
See that wounded face within us,
see it in each other's face,
see its truth in saints and sinners,
ours not to own but to embrace:
see it painted by a maiden,
artless past the power of thought,
humbly taken in a moment,
unpretentious and unwrought.

VII. JESUS FALLS A SECOND TIME

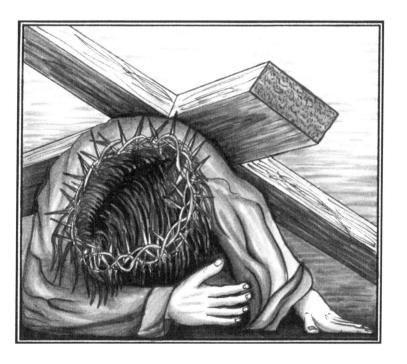

i.

Deaf!
I stumble and the outcast wood
strikes me on the ear
and all the street's liveliness retreats;
I see them shouting but I cannot hear.
Was ever sound so sweet
as now in the claustrophobic gloom,
dead, closed as the tomb?
I sometimes wondered when they brought a poor, deaf soul to me
if he might have been better without curses
and mean speech
but then I thought of the song of the wind in the trees,
the chant of the water on the pebbled beach,
the birds in the reeds
and, above all, the lullaby and the hurdy-gurdy.
I could watch the words
but I liked to hear the sound
of the intonation of a penitential psalm
and feel blood racing as Pharaoh's chariots drowned.
They walk jerkily,
as if looking round corners.
I have passed from a truculent sedition
into a dumb beast,
beaten past cognition.
Simon makes a sign that says
there is no more time,
movement is the only way to stem the blows.
I rise, shakily without a sense of balance,
amazed by the chaos of movement

robbed of its sense in silence.
"Up! Get up!"
I hear through the fog of bloody pounding.
"What! are you deaf, or something?"
The movements fall into patterns,
jerking limbs take on a sense of shape.
Better the cursing than the silence,
better the knowledge than the silent fear.
Was that you calling?
Yes, I thought it was.
I can hear.

ii.

Silence
enfolds me, and the world serene
sends me to prophets chanting in a wordless dream.
Silence lends intensity to their rocky faces,
hewn from the adversity of wild places,
etched with exile.
John was like that, always waiting for something,
always just thrown out of somewhere,
hammering to get back in.
You could guess the words from his arms
and the look on his listeners' faces,
short, sharp phrases
of sin and begin,
relent and repent,
die for the end is nigh.
Judaism is a worship of silence,
not enough to hear,

not enough to say,
more like a mantra than a drama.
I brace myself against a pillar
to bring words back:
I have had enough of the stark endeavour.
I have brought gracious music
and the sound of laughter and sweet words
instead of ashes to the altar.
The interlude ends in a burst of swearing,
a fair price for the beauty of sound.
I can hear the passion climbing in front of me,
wave upon wave of shallow rant,
a fair price for the heavenly chorus.
But amid the discord of the ragged chant,
I hear a bell ringing in a chandler's shop,
the hiss of beans poured from a sack into a measuring pan,
the clink of the weights in the silversmith's
and, oh, the laugh of secret love
after a secret kiss
behind a curtain.
I healed them for my Father
but I healed them for this,
to hear the world's torment and the world's bliss.

VIII. JESUS MEETS THE WOMEN OF JERUSALEM

i.

Women

weep not, the occasion is slight,

your saviour treads his way in the footsteps

    of countless prophesies;

comfort one another

as the day reaches its grisly height

and descends into decay;

comfort one another as you may,

until you see my promise kept on the third day.

Remember the fish you gutted on the shore,

remember the loved one who received a cure,

remember the good news for the poor;

remember the lifeless girl leaping

and the mother of Nain no longer weeping.

I have wept in secret, in quiet places,

in the night when those who caused me pain were sleeping;

I have wept for the doubt and the disbelief,

and the turning back when the road grew steep,

and the lust for glory,

and the way they thought I would change for them,

making all their sacrifices worthy.

But today I have done with weeping for them

and you, in turn, must cease weeping for me.

Weep, if you must,

for the city which killed the prophets

and see the pattern repeated

of repentance and falling away;

and weep because there is no end to it.

Just as these holy men have injured what is good,

have deliberately misunderstood,
do you think that your children will escape
    another deadly bout of destruction?
Look, see those noble stones,
can the Temple stand against the strength of God's command?
How many burnt bulls does it take,
to blot out a deliberate mistake?
Mothers of Jerusalem, weep not for me
but for yourselves and your posterity.

ii.

Goodly women,
weep not for such bliss,
weep not
for the small toils
on such a day as this.
Look,
where God leads his Christ must follow there,
with a gentle smile and a quiet prayer.
See past the wounds to the triumph of his will,
think of the signs and stages you have seen
from Cana's overflowing cups
to Lazarus' bursting tomb,
from the witty woman at Jacob's well
to foot washing in the upper room.
Yet there is much that calls for tears
that tears cannot assuage,
failure to see God's truth
and earth's terrible, treacherous rage
beginning with the Romans who lost patience with the Holy City,

and then the vengeance by those who claimed to follow me.
Weep for the tortured and the torturer,
for the down-trodden and the hollowness of tyranny;
weep for the dire betrayal of the brokenness you see.
Weep for my chosen people
and those marked out with the yellow star, for
the breach, with Stephen's death,
which led to Krystalnacht
and the near death of who we are,
for the comfortable churchiness which has subdued
the holy ground of penitence.
Women, women,
weep not for me, weep not as a reflex
overflowed then gone
but weep dry-eyed,
ceaselessly, for your part in my traduction,
a cruel seduction flowing from a people's hardened heart.
Goodly women, weep not for such bliss
but for the world unmade,
the sweetness gone amiss.

IX. JESUS FALLS A THIRD TIME

i.

Blinded!
A clot detaches, freeing the blood
which streams into my half closed eyes.
I sprawl across the cutting stones
into the mud
and lie momentarily numb.
O darkness, come.
I see the sun, flashing across the lake,
and the birds in the boat's wake
and silver fish in the pebbles;
and gaily coloured shawls hung out to dry;
and the dull glow of the grapes.
And amid the clash of colour and the
    infinite variety of perspective,
from the mountain to a pedlar's bead,
I see a drab man sitting, drained of vibrancy.
As I walk towards him he turns his head away
with an exaggerated twist.
"Is that," he says, "Jesus of Nazareth?"
"Yes, but do not worry yourself, old man,
the master is in a hurry
to tell a story
of how the poor shall be set free."
"But how true can it be if it doesn't include me?"
"A cheeky fellow," says Peter, almost brutally.
"The story can wait a moment.
I suppose you want to see?"
"Indeed I do.
I have heard of so many wonders,

I believe in you."
"Well, let us slip behind these bales and see
what we can do."
As he half shouts for joy I shout in pain,
another blow has fallen and my sight returns.
My eyes ache and the blood burns;
but the sharp field has shrunk into a dull point,
into an overwhelming idea,
to stand, to reach, to leave the pain behind,
to escape into the inward mind.

ii.

O world grown dim,
O hallowed, empty space
where sight saw the crooked, painful way,
free now to wander.
Stone-struck, I to kneel and say: "Father,
I offer you this final, kneeling prayer
to give me strength.
We are almost there."
I cannot help recalling the wrangling over the blind man
in the Temple, treated as if he had sinned,
an icon of evil,
all the hearings and swearings
and notaries and genealogies,
as if they could not recognise the good behind the healing.
This is why I am kneeling;
to banish the parched, adversarial law
and usher love's triumph through the Temple door.
They have known, since I overturned the tables,

what this would mean,
the end of the power,
the end of the machine,
the outbreak of innocence,
the freedom from duress;
I kneel for love here
as I have knelt before them in their holy fortress.
I think of the blindness of the blind man, and
        the blindness of the inquisition
and the blindness taught into so many good people;
and I remember Cousin John always asking:
"What did you come out to see?"
It was always about seeing.
Blindness is a peculiar curse
which is why I love those who stumble,
yet still follow;
and why I rest, blind now,
better to see the final triumph of my last journey.
O world grown dim,
let light flow from my core,
to lead where I am crowned for evermore.

X. JESUS IS STRIPPED OF HIS GARMENTS

i.

Naked!
Torn dignity and every wound laid bare:
the hands that broke bread now broken;
arms that blessed, too weak to reach;
the body that embraced, marked with the
    scourge's intimate prying;
legs that strode or sprang from ship to beach,
incapable of bearing.
But the point, sharper than thorn and flay,
is the out-lawing as they would say,
from God's community.
And yet,
it is a fitting culmination of a lifetime of leaving
the body and the heart open.
This is the moment when degradation is invoked
to separate the body from the human,
as a necessary precondition for destruction;
that a man must die for the people
we must ensure that he is a piece of derision
too low for cruelty.
But what would it be for, this dignity,
this protection?
There never was a need; and is not now.
They have simply made explicit what has always been implicit:
there are no limits to the ways in which the God made man for us
will relate to the human condition;
it is not just an abstract kenosis
but one of blood and bone
of dignity and raiment;

it is the apogee of 'reality';
incarnation, the opposite of a theory.
The baby is a necessary beginning
and this 'reversion' - as Job might say -
is as necessary an ending.
Almost out of the range of the human,
not from degradation but from the anticipation of completion,
all that remains of the body is its pain.

ii.

In the beginning
The Word was made flesh and dwells on Calvary.
Look upon The Word, not a demi God from Olympus
nor an athlete oiled and primed for glory
but what is left of a man when humanity has done its worst
and failed.
This disrobing, God unveiled,
is the supposed last stage of derision,
the final assertion of human authority,
the sign that there is no way back,
that the scapegoat has been cast out of the city.
Yet what you see is the failure to subvert the prophesy.
They are not so much malefactors as unknowing collaborators;
they are party to a glorious collusion.
The dice roll for what they have taken
but the Father has already determined how they will come to rest.
Prophets have walked naked for me
and now I stand naked at the end of that sequence of history
which began with Adam putting on his fig-leaf;
we are in a state of transition

but they are still working in the old dispensation.
Their rage is almost blown out,
their achievements suddenly dwindle,
and they will soon wonder what it was all about,
passing through history
from self-justifying hysteria to necessary wisdom.
Better you see the bones and the wounds and the brokenness
than think it was all an illusion;
better to be called The Word made flesh
than the one who said he was.
They have done their worst;
and it never was going to be
bad enough to stop me loving,
for nothing could be.

XI. JESUS IS CRUCIFIED

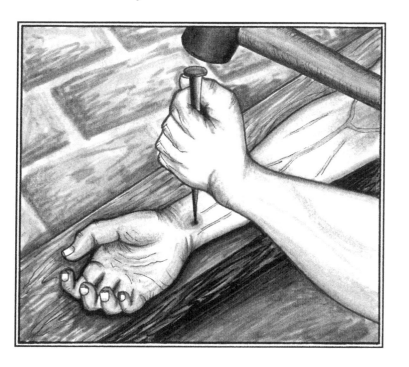

i.

Help!
Most pain I have taken quietly
but a coarse nail hacked through the hand
slices a nerve,
breaks my reserve
when I thought that pain had reached its constant pitch.
Not from a selfish perspective,
I wonder about such a casual infliction
as if cruelty were necessary to preserve surface tranquillity,
as if my brothers and sisters were wild beasts,
as if we had learned no kindness as God's children.
What could these men have done to deserve death?
One is so driven beyond endurance
that he can only resent
but, like mine, his offence is surely hardly worthy of comment;
the other admits to something
but, again, death probably makes it seem
        disproportionately awful.
The infractions and codifications seem so trivial,
which is why I came,
to break My Father's people from their legalist addiction,
to teach them to remember love and pain.
There is, then, a terrible irony
that the law-destroyer should be destroyed by the law,
that the charge of blasphemy should be made against me.
I wonder how long;
I wish it were quiet;
I forgive the man who asks and the one who will not
and at last the pain begins to act as its own anaesthetic.

I see women standing like distant figures at the edge of the lake,
watching the boats come in.
The horizon wavers in mist
and the water and the women are momentarily sharp,
and then an illusion.
How long?
The soldiers wonder how long.
All we want now is for the waiting to be over
before something else goes wrong.

ii.

High
above the crowd I see the Temple smeared with golden stains
shining
in the sun;
the cognoscenti and the curious squint at the inscription
and then the light drains;
the air, once filled with paschal bleating,
grows thin and still,
as the fatal night in Egypt is remembered in day-time darkness,
and the elders, so careful, have not daubed
    lamb's blood on the lintels
of the Temple which must fall.
The Angel of The Lord has come to dwell
on this shabby hill
where I have been lifted high,
to triumph and to die.
This unaccustomed darkness makes everyone uneasy,
as they have been since the beginning.

Whereas they have apparently orchestrated
     events leading to my humiliation,
they have bumped and edged their way,
grasping at what I have left them;
and now they just want it to be over
for, from beginning to end, it has been an untidy affair,
offending their love of the clean and the elegant.
Once the nails were driven in and the cross made secure,
everybody wanted to be gone
but then came the darkness
and they are rooted in agonised indecision.
They do not remember the instructions to Moses
and the passage of the Angel of Death in the darkness;
they do not remember the sun-dial turned backwards;
they do not remember exile.
Except for the power of priesthood
and the comfort of ritual, they have forgotten everything.
High above,
I am still their remembering.

XII. JESUS DIES ON THE CROSS

i.

Dying
is an unfamiliar falling
away of the limbs and the will,
an ebbing of purpose and momentum;
pain and exhaustion flicker
so that there is a strange alternation
between being in oneself and watching;
and with this withering, what is left of life's
    flower turns towards my Father.
I 'cross off' the world
in asking forgiveness for all who are left in witness,
I ask him - partly to escape the pain,
more to achieve completeness -
to take me back into his arms.
"Have I done enough?"
I wonder, peering back out into the world of darkness;
and this uncertainty makes me feel unutterably desolate.
I think: "Has he abandoned me?"
but then I see a shadowy drama played out,
half-way between earth and heaven,
as the spirit of Elijah and an angel hover over a beggar.
A goblet of wine glints dully in the gloom,
and there is a macabre dance
between a Levite and a soldier.
The spirits of the thieves flash by like comets
and I think that is when I begin to die
as the impetus for speculation fades.
I am sure some think it is the last moment of desolation,
the ruin of The Kingdom,

or perhaps one man's humiliation;
and others, improbably, will think
that behind the 'scandal' of my degradation
there is something deep and golden;
but there is nothing.
The essence of obedience is to live in my Father's space,
humble, unconditional.

ii.

Time
quickens as the blood ebbs.
Time for final dispositions.
I say: "Mother."
She says: "Sweet Jesus mine,
soon you will have gone back to the Father,
    to your golden throne."
"Mother, I will not leave you to earthly trials for long
between my throne and your throne,
only to see The Spirit and my work for God well done,
to see the Spirit transform my beloved companions.
I give you John
for muscle and for bone."
She looks nervously as a woman would
who moves from the household she has built
to a bachelor's retreat.
I say: "John, here is your mother
in need of comfort and protection;
give her some leeway in the matter of lentils and linen."
He looks slightly guilty, the state of the place worrying him,
even while this sacred drama is reaching its climax.

They stand, not quite looking, not quite touching,
not quite knowing how to behave in this new situation.
The rest draw into a circle
and, in memory of our last meal together,
I call for a cup
and, even though it is more like vinegar than wine,
it serves the purpose,
the memory is distilled,
the Scriptures are fulfilled.
This is the last human act I undertake;
and that circle is the last human scene I see.
Now all dispositions have been made,
the drama is completed.
The Father has been glorified in me;
he holds what they would call my future, in his hands
to which I travel as time ceases to pray
and the blood ebbs away.

XIII. THE BODY OF JESUS IS TAKEN DOWN FROM THE CROSS

i.

Empty
of spirit, empty of blood,
some Pharisees say we shall all rise at the end of time
but we are more practical;
only our lives of devotion and sacrifice - forgive
the phrase -
are of 'any use' to our God.
He, who cured the sick and raised the dead,
who calmed the winds and ruled the fish,
who cheered the crowds,
is nothing.
As for The Kingdom he foresaw, who is to carry on?
So much of what he said was enigmatic,
even provisional,
as if he knew something of himself beyond the normal,
but we are broken,
we are like the leaves that crackle on the Autumn fire,
we are preparing to go into exile,
we have resiled from the immortal.
From being the purest person ever known
he is now unclean;
who shall carry him
once the soldiers make him over?
We will not choose, we will not isolate
ourselves
but all will share in his contamination,
the last touch of what changed us forever,
in the hope that we may hang onto something,
in the hope that something startling will change within us;

in the hope that we will realise something spectacular
in what he said to us.
Mary begins to cry,
then stops,
singing something half-way between a dirge
and a lullaby
as we lay the broken body in her arms.
Strange bread to feed a mother,
the son she once fed.

ii.

Pierced,
emptied as Simeon foretold,
a light to the Gentiles beckoning.
Ecce Homo,
the man who would be king,
is taken from his place on high
and laid on earth.
I watch them as they wait for permission
to take charge of the corpse,
wanting to get on, frightened of the unnatural dark,
of the Romans, the Priests and of Passover coming on.
Joseph arrives with an instruction
and Nicodemus, for once, moves out of the shadows.
I watch them carry me who carried them
in a slightly hurried procession;
my Chosen People have never had a taste
        for death as a culmination.
And then I see the whole world from Adam to the end,
each person born to live forever

in the Father's love;
how this shall be I do not know,
although I am the means.
"The Word made flesh"
always was a mystery to me
and now I am in limbo,
looking down,
waiting for something to happen.
They walk, slightly awkwardly,
although I weigh next to nothing,
into a tiny garden,
so close to but different from the dump of Golgotha.
John looks at my mother,
carefully closing the gate,
at once achieving tidiness and privacy.
A slave appears with a cask of embalming unguent
and I suddenly cease to be an object of pity
but of intense attention
which temporarily drives away the heart's cold
but I see it creeping back,
remembering Simeon;
and I long to be able to say something
but the God that comes from timelessness into time
bides my time.

XIV. JESUS IS PLACED IN THE TOMB

i.

Un-space!
There is no narrower place than a tomb,
no place to go, no room to grow;
bones and a shadow.
Tidy but unfinished, the miserable cargo
is stowed in the unforgiving maw,
the fearsome hold,
eternal cold.
The wounds are dressed,
the eyes are closed,
the linen masks the mess,
giving the appearance of normality, of wholesomeness.
The prayers are hurried but the grief is long,
a frightened farewell,
and a sad song.
The bond of ritual breaks
and the air grows desperate:
"Where shall we go?
Where shall we go now?
What shall we do?
It grows late!
He has gone; and the world moves on.
Even mourners eat.
Those who fled, how will they be?
Can they be comforted with bread?
It is not ours to judge, to rebuke,
to say something to them he never would have said.
We have performed in the office of women,
watching, wailing and remembering.

We have performed in the office of a woman,
mending, soothing and recovering,
making the best of things,
covering up the cracks with a clean display."
They close the gate
and hurry down the darkening street,
with angels, newly landed,
listening to their echoing feet.
Soldiers on night watches rarely bother to do more
than file a report which says nothing happened
which, as the angels, in all respects, keep their distance,
is properly accurate.
The soldiers sleep,
the angels wait,
no foot comes near the tiny gate.

ii.

O necessary resting place,
this cool, hospitable tomb,
receive my bones as earth disposes,
sweet with the balm of marginally guilty affection.
Make good the broken,
enshroud the head,
ensure the tidiness peculiar to the dead,
so fraught while living.
Welcome me to my temporary home,
a concentrated space
which, if they stopped to remember, would
    focus their wild longings,
gathering their despair into a place for prayer.

It was never a case of earthly disappearance
nor the spectacular departure of Elijah:
there always was a time and a tomb;
three days of waiting before the fulfilment of the promise.
And then there was the 'game' of time over Lazarus.
Surely they could have made something of it.
You might say that I was unnecessarily enigmatic,
impossible to de-code;
but I hardly knew myself;
I hardly knew my self.
All is now gathered of The Word Made Flesh,
signs and discourses,
smiles and disputes, into this tiny space.
The hands that washed their feet,
that broke their bread,
that blessed with palms upon their head,
are still;
the heart that beat for them,
with pain so sharp and sweet,
that fluttered when they fell,
that welcomed like a well,
has ceased its generous beat;
the ears that heard sweet music and sharp taunts,
the prayer and the imprecation,
are released;
the eyes that saw the beauty of the Father's earth,
its human tarnish and its human worth,
are closed.
All incarnational resources are transposed
from that unequalled flesh into eternal grace.
O necessary resting place.

Lightning Source UK Ltd.
Milton Keynes UK
UKOW06f0128270216

269214UK00010B/86/P